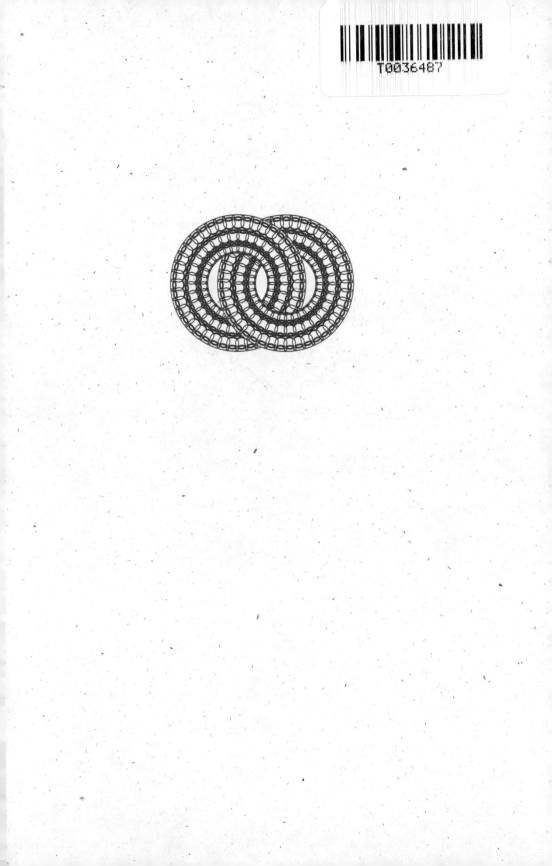

Deep Are These
Distances Between Us

Deep Are These Distances Between Us

Susan Atefat-Peckham

Edited and with a Foreword
by Darius Atefat-Peckham

CAVANKERRY
PRESS

CavanKerry Press Ltd.
Fort Lee, New Jersey
www.cavankerrypress.org

Publisher's Cataloging-in-Publication Data
provided by Five Rainbows Cataloging Services
Names: Atefat-Peckham, Susan, 1970-2004, author. | Atefat-Peckham, Darius, writer of foreword.
Title: Deep are these distances between us / Susan Atefat-Peckham ; foreword by Darius Atefat-Peckham.
Description: Fort Lee, NJ : CavanKerry Press, 2023.
Identifiers: ISBN 978-1-933880-96-9 (paperback)
Subjects: LCSH: Poets, American—21st century. | Poets, Iranian—21st century. | Women immigrants. | Feminism. | Families. | Spirituality. | BISAC: POETRY / Women Authors. | POETRY / Middle Eastern. | POETRY / Subjects & Themes / Family.
Classification: LCC PS3601.T44 D44 2023 (print) | LCC PS3601.T44 (ebook) | DDC 811/.6—dc23.

Cover artwork: Maryam Lamei Harvani
Cover and interior text design by Ryan Scheife, Mayfly Design
First Edition 2023, Printed in the United States of America

CAVANKERRY
PRESS

 Made possible by funds from the
New Jersey State Council on the Arts, a partner
agency of the National Endowment for the Arts.

 arts.gov

CavanKerry Press is grateful for the support it receives from
the New Jersey State Council on the Arts, the National
Endowment for the Arts, and the New Jersey Arts and
Culture Renewal Fund.

In addition, CavanKerry Press gratefully acknowledges
generous grants and emergency support received during the
COVID-19 pandemic from the following funders:

The Academy of American Poets

Community of Literary Magazines and Presses

National Book Foundation

New Jersey Council for the Humanities

New Jersey Economic Development Authority

Northern New Jersey Community Foundation

The Poetry Foundation

US Small Business Administration

Also by Susan Atefat-Peckham

That Kind of Sleep (Coffee House Press, 2001)
Talking Through the Door (Syracuse University Press, 2014)

for all those who loved her

Contents

Foreword

My childhood was defined by distances and what lay between them. I found this, my mother's second poetry manuscript, in a bin saved by my grandmother of all of my mother's documents: thousands of printed emails, drafts of children's books and various manuscripts, saved rejection and acceptance letters, and various other forms of correspondence, hardly any of it addressed to me. *I must get rid of all this stuff,* Bibi whispered beside me. For once, I understood my grandparents' inability to rid themselves of even the most everyday things Susie left behind. I felt an urgency to read everything, to take what I needed, and to make something of it, *to speak of /and hold, to carry, to keep.* I snatched up this manuscript and held it like it might disappear, like it might be taken from me. I began reading.

I didn't grow up communing with the dead. My mother had been absent from my dreams my entire life. I yearn for her, for my Iranian heritage, for understanding. Even now, I feel profound jealousy when my grandma, Bibi, tells me a cardinal appears each time she moves to the porch to light a cigarette, or when someone says they spoke to my mother in a dream, and *it was so real, so good, seeing her again.* I was just three years old when she and my older brother died, returning from the Red Sea, where we'd gone for the day. A day I don't remember, let alone revisit in dream. It was easier for me to dismiss Bibi's dreams as projections on the part of one who survived the accident, rather than a reaching out from the world beyond.

Or at least that's what I believed until I began reading my mother's writing. I found that even in death, however distant, she was timely and multifaceted. With the discovery of each new manuscript, I inexplicably found the versions of her I longed for in the exact moments that I needed her. In her diaries, an imperfect, obsessive teenager and young adult; in her creative nonfiction, a caring and considerate orator of her own body and soul; in her children's books, a loving mother; and in her poetry, a woman wracked with joy and grief trying desperately to remember and represent what's been lost, to breathe new life. A woman reaching out. *Nothing / dies in places we've left behind,* she writes. The guilt, the pain, the praise and joy—it's all here, as if in conversation with how I, myself, feel about her.

What's most impressive, however, and what you'll find in these pages, is my mother's resilience, her nurture and care even despite her situation or circumstance, a nurture that persists beyond the grave. My mother grew up transnationally, born in New York, spending her teenage years in Switzerland and visiting Iran in her childhood before settling in the United States. The person you'll think and breathe alongside in these pages is an Iranian woman of the diaspora, who, with her parents, experienced the Iranian Revolution and the oppressive measures veiling expression of Iranian femininity and womanhood, as well as the turmoil of the Iran–Iraq War throughout the 1980s. A woman who, living in the United States following the attacks of 9/11, brokenheartedly witnessed the ensuing Islamophobia and fear of the Middle East as she began a family of her own and became a mother, as she began to think about how to answer the difficult questions her children would be sure to ask her as they experienced racism for the first time. A woman who devoted her life to answering these difficult questions, and whose work resulted in this: a treatise on the expression of love, empathy, and compassion, a work that embodies those terms set by Sa'adi in his poem "Bani Adam," or "Sons of Adam," translated by Dick Davis and inscribed on a carpet hung in the United Nations, her father's place of work:

Man's sons are parts of one reality
Since all have sprung from one identity;
If one part of a body's hurt, the rest
Cannot remain unmoved and undistressed;
If you're not touched by others' pain, the name
Of "man" is one you cannot rightly claim.

At the time of her death, Susie's work was transitioning into a more spiritual realm, one informed by her interest in Sufism and by her long absence from her ancestral home due to political tensions between the American and Iranian governments that made it unsafe for her to travel there—making her miss, among other family gatherings, her beloved grandfather's funeral. She found, in Sufism and Sufi poetics, an alternate form of travel both physical and metaphysical, a kind of music that touched her poetic ear and soul with an intimacy that transcends borders, and a sect of Islam that made space for deviants, dissidents, intellectuals, and all those whose identities are rejected by the societal constructs engrained in the state religion. She fell in love with Sufi poets such as Hafez, Rumi, Attar, and Sa'adi, and delighted in seeing their work of sprawling human empathy and spirituality reflected in English-language contemporary poets who challenged and pushed forward their ideas.

In an interview with *Poets & Writers* just following the publication of her first book, *That Kind of Sleep* (Coffee House Press, 2001), Susie expanded on the roles of familial love and religion in her new work:

The family—the children especially—are the most important part of our culture, besides the religion. The religion accentuates the closeness of the family as well. Because I was writing out of absence, my poetry brought people I hadn't seen in a long time back to me. In the poems I can make them come back to life. I can put the words in their mouths; I can see them moving again.

Every time someone reads that poem, every time I read
that poem, these people are there. In many ways I think
I wrote this book to fill the spaces between us.

Religion and spirituality for Susie were inextricable from fa-
milial intimacy and regeneration, or continuation, of ancestral
voice. For this reason, distance manifests in a myriad of ways in
her work, always with nuance and complexity.

An issue of paramount importance to my mother was that
of women's rights in Iran: the distance and hypocrisy in how the
patriarchal Islamic state treats women, especially in the period
just following the 1979 revolution. In her poem "Tara," Susie
imagines her cousin waiting in prison for her sentence, punished
for submitting to love and subject to the state's cruel double stan-
dards. She writes of how her cousin's perception changes and os-
cillates under this unjust treatment:

> the bars must look to her like the very lines
> of memory, or music, or the passageways
> between long legs, or the distances between
> parallel lives, carefully measured, like comfort,
> and obedience, and it doesn't matter anymore
> what is said or what is left to be said, because
> she thinks if she really tries she can make herself
> disappear into the spaces between them . . .

The *spaces between* have multivalent usages in Susie's work
and her thinking. They are at once spaces to be filled and to be
disappeared into. Threatening yet brimming with potential. By
the poem's end, the woman of the poet's imagination is one in
necessary conflict with the divine as it's used to justify unjust
persecution, articulating the distance and difference between
morals and what is *right*, between a constructed and cruel God
and a divine presence or religion as *closeness*. This conflict is
what allows her to reach across those spaces, those distances, and

touch the minds and spirits of future generations, including the poet herself.

> her prison,
> a rifle, or a reed, a child, or, even, God, who
> says one thing I hear a long while, *I made*
> *the moral choice.*
> I say, *the right choice?*
> when the bars, the bars are not enough to punish
> us clean, to close us in, to hold us back.

This distance between a man's and a woman's right to self-expression is a tension and fixity Susie's work aims to address. Even in the Sufi religion, women in Iran are denied the right to dance publicly, in the expression of human and divine interconnectedness that is Dervish whirling. Incredibly, in this manuscript, we see Susie's aims *to fill the spaces between us* come to fruition by way of her poetic voice, refusing to let the bars *hold us back.* She creates space for her beloveds to whirl, to dance—she creates true revolution, both in the human body's ability to mimic the earth in its turning around the sun, and in the more topical sense of the word, allowing radical love to triumph over hate.

This love, if it asserts itself in a world that seems to lack the capacity for it, becomes a form of resistance. *We are too connected not to care too / much for one another,* she writes. *Deep Are These Distances Between Us* transcends the depths of division, the oppressive distance between herself and her beloved heritage, speaking to and speaking *back* her ancestors, both those who have been lost and those who are sure to survive.

My father tells me I once asked him this question in my car seat while we were driving many hours to visit my grandparents or the woman who would become my second mother: *Daddy, can we take an airplane to see Mommy and Cyrus in heaven?*

Now, nearly nineteen years later, I can't say if I believe in an afterlife of any kind. I don't know if I'll ever have a relationship with my mother and brother beyond the one I've forged for my-self, her mystical presence in poetry and art. I grew up immersed in fantasy worlds, traversing space and time, trying to escape from my own tragic origins. What I found within these worlds was a gateway to my own reality much more precise than I could have ever imagined. I found that I do believe in the power of story to tell truths unknowable, to reach out and connect.

And with this discovery comes another: since my mother was a poet endlessly speaking out to the void, is it so crazy to think that she might be able to speak *from* it? Or that perhaps in life she inhabited a space only true artists can, what one of my favorite writers, Mark Doty, calls *more miraculous than any ghost: an intervention in reality committed by the power of art.* Is it so crazy to believe that I, too, might go there?

> Going back, there were many spaces—the cultural distances, the linguistic distances. When I write the poems, I am trying to bring us together in some space that is sacred to me. We all exist in our ancestors and our spirits are very much from our ancestors. I'm interested in discovering what that is—which parts of us are from the past.

So, when she claims, in these poems, *I'm sure I / know how I will die, the pull of thighs, / tearing through tangles of leaves,* I don't doubt her prophecy for a second. Don't we all die this way—forever and refusing its finality, again and again and again? This is the world she has created, and deftly she moves her way back through it, blessing me time and again with a language that transcends time, borders, and even death. Throughout my life thus far, my mother's poetry, and poetry in general, has given me something to learn from and believe in. I believe in her love for her family and children. I believe in love made, through the sprawling tradition of Persian mystics, boundless and eternal. As my father wrote to me in the original note to this manuscript,

There is no airplane to heaven, but poetry is the vessel of the soul. Here is your mother, right here.
I've never believed anything more.

Darius Atefat-Peckham
May 2022
Huntington, West Virginia

the future courses
through the beating heart, over, and over,
keeping time.
Pushing through blue
burning water, to sky, through torn seams
of membranes, we burst from the deep,
dark black mouth of memory.

—Susan Atefat-Peckham, 1970–2004

Smuggling: An Essay

i.

When the plane landed, I walked back to my seat. By then, the backs of women's heads twisted with cloth, tight and smoothed over, revealing skull shapes, round, long, square, knobbed; they seemed like hundreds of pillars rising each from the back of a chair. The transformation was stunning. Even in their faces, now meek. When I walked down the aisle to the restroom a few minutes earlier, facing the passengers, women brightened with worn lipstick and curled hair, arms sleeveless, legs bare, miniskirted. The papers in my hand shuffled by them— the rise and fall of their Kleenex, wiping, chadors, and scarves paralleled my own hurry. We seemed like crows in a birdbath, the curled rise of paper in the air, a cleansing of face, a quick scurry of fingernail and acetone, a black fluttering. I forgot that I brought my manuscript with me. It was a habit to bring it everywhere I traveled. Now, en route to Iran and near landing, I rushed to the restroom, ripped my words, and flushed them down.

I thought of my great-uncle Atefat with his mellifluous voice and old poems, and I wondered where my words would wind up, imagined them dissolving in a blue tank at the belly of the aircraft, winding in urine and excrement, dirtied water and soap scum. Mother had spotted my manuscript in my carry-on and had convinced me to do it, saying to Father, "Look." Then shaking her head and rolling her eyes. "Look what she brought."

Government workers in Tehran airport would not have been so understanding. Had they seen that I was a writer, they would have detained us for hours of questioning. I had nothing to hide. But no one cared for the waiting, the questions, the prying. As I stood above the bowl and ripped the pages, I recalled the moment in some European movie when the protagonist ripped her

1

passport and flushed it down. I remembered the revolutionary executions of 1979, when I was still a child, and I thought of my grandparents and cousins, aunts and uncles, good law-abiding citizens who never questioned their lives—or their governments—one of my cousins having been captured on the battlefield by Iraqis while rescuing the injured. He was never seen again.

When it is your country, there is loyalty.

"What are you doing bringing that here and jeopardizing your family?" Father had said over the rise and fall of cloth. I didn't consider my work subversive. Still, I imagined Grandfather frantic at the airport had we been detained.

Mother added, "That's bad."

In the bathroom, I held the sink, braced myself for landing. The blue antibacterial water swirled over my sentences, lines, the paragraphs, the stanzas tearing down their middles, the thoughts stopping at midline, the words ripping to blue letters, turning, sticking to the silver bowl, turning, dying blue. Sucking in, out loud. When no words were left, the sucking stopped. And the bottom of the bowl snapped shut.

ii.

I would never grow accustomed to the buses now separating men and women. To the silence of people. The chador I was forced to wear. The quiet I was forced to keep. And all that absence. The cousin "still away at war," now fifteen years. Almost five years passed since the war ended. Still, our family waits for him to round the bend of our road, see his head rise over the windowsill, see themselves jump in the samovar's reflection, elated, the edge of his eyebrow looking at them from around the doorframe. He would stand at the threshold for a moment, his arms hanging limp at his sides, his hands square at the ends. Then rush to his mother, now fifteen years older. She would fix him *sharbat*, a cherry syrup drink, sweet, cloying, tell him how she never lost hope. Even when the others had. Even when they looked at her askance after the radio announced all Iraqi prisoners of war had been freed—and he was still not home. The spoon would knock the glass as she stirred the rose-tinted drink, the high-pitched clanking reminding her, this was no dream, this was no sleep— *he is home.* Inside, the syrup would jump and swirl, blush the water. The glass would be cool and wet but his fingertips warm as they brushed her hands when she handed him the drink. *My boy,* she would think. It would be summer. And he would be bearded nonetheless—a good Muslim. The roses would be full in the garden, the children splashing in the *jube* outside, laughing. It would be just this way, when he came home. She had it all figured out. Except he never came. And she is still waiting. Even now.

My parents once listed those who died since they had emigrated from Iran almost forty years ago. They listed over thirty. At least eight since my last visit. Naneh Jan, Hamid, Ameh Nosrat, Ameh Jan, Grandfather, Amoo Reza, Ameh Massoud, Amoo Atefat, and Reza. Old age, war disappearance, bone cancer, heart attack, execution. Not there to witness the change, I can imagine them alive. I can write them alive. But that would not change facts. There are many ways to become absent. This is what happens when one leaves a place for too long. This is what happens when one waits for too long. The world is not never–never land. Things change.

When I last left Isfahan, Great-Uncle Atefat was still alive, holding his four-hundred-year-old books and singing poetry. He sang something by Hafiz, and looked to me for a reaction. I stared at him, my eyes blank. He took a drag from his cigarette and winced. He was smaller than I had remembered, old and frail in body, white haired, but mostly bald, fair skinned.

He leaned to my father next to him while looking at me and, as if I wouldn't understand, said, "She's forgotten the words. She doesn't understand the words. Doesn't understand." Exhaled the smoke. "Forgotten the words—*hayfe.*" A shame. Then smiled lightly.

When I last left Tehran, Grandfather was still alive in the

hallway. Grandmother poured the water and rose petals over the threshold, into the red street dust. It was an old Persian tradition to ensure safe travels and a quick return. As the water ran the length of the street, it collected the dust, becoming a dry dust animal creeping to the gutter. I saw that much from the rear-view window. I saw Grandfather turn slowly for the gate, wipe his face. I saw Grandmother adjust her chador over her brow, tighten the cloth, tighten her arms, and move to the center of the road to see us round the bend. Even once we disappeared, I imagined she stood for a while, a black pillar, which soon turned and walked through the emptiness we left behind.

iii.

In the aircraft on the way home, I thought of the last-minute scene we had caused at the airport, trying to bring over some candles I sculpted. They said they would not allow paraffin, a bomb-making material, on the aircraft. I spent weeks learning from my cousin, days laboring over these candles, burning my fingers on the wax petals and flame, molding, melting, shaping, and I half-suspected that the reason they wanted to confiscate them was to enjoy them in their own homes. Wild with the moment, I snatched the candles from the guards, and placed them on the ground, my foot raised, ready to crush. They would not have my laboring.

"*Sabr kon!*" Wait, Mother said.

She remembered my father had not yet gone through the men's line, then passed the candles over the barrier to my aunt, who knew what to do. When Father walked toward us at the gate, he carried a garbage bag and grinned broadly.

They were now smuggled under the seat in front of me, and no one was the wiser. When the plane took off and Tehran disappeared beneath us, women unwrapped, breathed heavily, fanned themselves dry. They sprayed perfume on their necks, on their chests, dabbed rouge on their cheeks, chattered in loud boldness to one another about plans to visit a daughter in Germany, a son in the United States. I thought of reuniting with my American boyfriend, soon to be fiancé, soon to be husband. I thought of Mother, smuggling my engagement ring in a dirtied Kleenex. The female guards frisked her but didn't think to check her hands. Even in the commotion over the candles, we had looked at each other, remembering the ring, as they waved her through. I thought of all that noise—the chattering, the yelling, the weeping, the waiting, the changing. And, in the back of my mind, of music. Of my great-uncle singing Hafiz. Of my cousin giving me his book of Farsi poetry despite my illiteracy. Of my aunt still dreaming of her son returning home from the war. It is all there is left to do. I held the old book in my lap and thought of the silence we left behind, of how living there is quiet now, of how time might change people, mend living. I thought of all the bits of poems, the bits of stories, belly-up, the words perhaps still visible in the septic tank of some other foreign aircraft.

Night Conversations

Star said to Palm: How far
would I fall to your knots
and root? *Palm said:* Thousands
will kneel before you.

Star: I am
just white dust behind rippling
firelight.

Palm: See how
my green blades wear you
like rings.

Star: What will I do,
erased at sunrise?

Palm: Breathe
from my temple.

Star: How
do you see my burning path
yet not my face?

Palm: How
do you beg to travel such
unknown distances?

Star: Friend,
clap the blades of your leaves
into these black hours, for deep
are these distances between us.

I: Appearances

I ached from separation.
I cloaked myself in night,
emerged a shining moon.

Consumed in Love's fire,
I slip through any opening.
I rise like smoke.

—Rumi

Small Things

In the summer of morning
prayer, I hear Ghossam's friend
outside my window, scream-
singing, *Khordeh-riz na-dari?*
Ghablemeh ya ghashogh na-dari?
It is dawn. And this tinker boy always
wakes us at five a.m. begging
for small pots, spoons, things to keep.
I complain to Aunt Lili—it is her
house I sleep in—can't he collect
the dented and useless after
breakfast? In the Alborz mountains
the dervish curls his sleep around
his spoon, his boiling pot, tea
cup, axe, the blade gleaming
with first sunlight aside
on the ground in the shadow
of the round of his hip. The stone
sees his pelvis dip to the landscape
as if it became some far-off hill.
From the distant mountain
prison patching the breast of the hill
with barbed wire fencing, prisoners
cry. For life? Prayer? Music?
Mother hears them while we walk
through the cherry trees of a house
Father talks about buying. *Not*
here, she says. Too many voices
fill the wall a villager builds around
his home with stone and mortar,
adding layer on layer. *He is crazy,*
they say. Not to me. Why not?

Wall the spaces around our lives,
keep sound and life and age away?
And below in the valley, the boy
stands at a city suburb door, quiet
with negotiation, the dark spaces
of the house open to the street.
At the screen door Lili props open,
he widens the mouth of his bag
to receive the small glinting metal,
pans, pots, cups, spoons. He
becomes the god of small things,
saying, look at these small
uses entering the deep throat
of possession. How remarkable
the small are, not to bend
into shape but to speak of
and hold, to carry, to keep.

How to Get to the House on Takhti Street

        Walk uphill on Pahlavi Avenue.
Turn left on the alley that aches with stray
cats, and follow the stucco walls two blocks.
Make certain you've turned before you reach
the city bus stop once shut down for mass
revolutionary executions, not the backfire
of gasoline ignition but the squeezed trigger
clipping the streets

past the bazaar vendors burning ears
of corn, past the ribbed dogs that rock
their barreled bodies lifting and dropping
into the gutters, past the hungry desperation
of limbless beggars

where your hands will pull at the seams
of your empty pockets, where you'll hear
Nina screaming even before you see her
standing outside the gate, Grandmother inside,
Nina's arms, washed for morning prayers, still
dripping silver, her hands cupped like a bowl
filled with sunlight and water and pleading:

To get to this house on Takhti Street, think
of what it means to lose your father, think
of what it means to be left behind, think
of the scream so loud it comes out in silent
bowls shimmering with the hands of those who
survive.

Clean

                                 He's already
in the ground, Father says, his grief
wound in static. My son kicks
in my womb, two weeks from birth,
not enough room. I hear instead

Grandfather's voice from Tehran, *Dastet-*
o-beshoor, Wash your hands. Wash
your hands, and see
                  the razor, the brush,
the soap, the mornings I woke at dawn
and found him sitting in roses, ready
for prayer, facing west, legs bent, hands
turning over and over each other
like domed mosques, circling his chin,
his cheeks. An arc of silver cleans his jaw.
And hands gleam to torn edges of bread,
a cherry preserve on each flat wedge
bleeding red into the asphalt.
                         It is time
to pray, he would say, his hands washed
and raised. When songs of morning
prayer streaked his arms, he bowed
into sunlight.
                        And I
wonder how busy I must have been at noon
when Mother called Nebraska saying, *Talk*
to Grandpa. Talk to Grandpa. Fast. And I
was thinking of the place I needed to be
instead, already late, not knowing this
was it. The dying don't wait. Later,
she told me about the surgery, said when

I called he stood in a pool of manure.
Dried blood you know. From the wound
that cancer carved in his throat. Never healed.
She stopped. *He was shamed,* she said. *You
know how clean your grandfather always
was.* In some still world lay the brush, razor,
bowl of water heaving its surface with sun
and soap, his hands, praying
                              palms
facing Mecca, a red sky, *La ila ha illalah,*
knees snapped to the earth.
          Nine months
pregnant, the unborn wrapped in flesh
fabrics, heart beating, I imagine his arms
underground, wound in muslin, a clean
shaven face sticking from a cloth window,
his mustache bristled white, the rest
of him wrapped as tradition would have it,
in cotton. I imagine his fingers bent
beneath the threads, cherry preserve stain
in his nails, the tips meeting his thumbs,
red silent mouths, opening.
                              Grandfather,
I have washed my hands, I have
washed my hands, I have washed
my hands.

Ghossam Remembers His Brother

Somewhere from
Zaranj to Tehran, Ghossam's brother
rolls from the top of the bus into
dust, no money to ride in a seat
inside, no money for a decent
Muslim burial. Ghossam begs
for coins for his brother. His friend
will share small pieces
of metal.
He says, *One day
I will buy a knife—no, one day,
I will buy a gun and stand
on a car and shoot everyone.*
He says, *One day I will kill
all Iranians.* Esmat Khanoom
wonders which village he came
from in Afghanistan. She knows
this kid has no one, and feeds him
sholeh zard, watches the tip
of his spoon dip into the saffron
and pistachio design, cutting
the surface of the pudding, listens
to him speak through the yellow
gelatin clinging to his teeth.

Hats

Agha Rashid and Agha Shaheen find
cut shapes of tough wool in the trash
out front, too tough for filling pillows.
They wonder, What had it been?
Why all these pieces? Unwanted
shoulder pads from a coat? Parts
of gardening gloves? Parts of a *lohaf-
korsi* gone bad?

                Was it the lover gone
mad, deciding it was time to part, then
cutting the blanket to bits as he walked
to the mountains one morning, thinking
to leave the pieces behind him like bread
crumbs, a path homeward, but no, instead
disappeared for days, as he had before,
always returning? Or was it punishment
to a child by his father for stealing sugar
cubes at the mosque? *We do not steal
from God. This sugar is holy.*

            What drives any of us to tear
a possession to bits? *It must be the lohaf-
korsi,* they decide, because lovers
are everywhere. They imagine the fire kettle
at its center, its blanket pulled taut
around it, a woolen wheel of warmth,
everyone together beneath it, hot chins
tucked into its circumference, the lengths
of their bodies like spokes, a small
universe with fire at the center.

                  They pluck
the pieces from the bag, slip them in
their pockets, never noticing the tiny

white tag with a number at its center
or the way the sun heats the shadow
between wool and hair.

Faces

                    Mother traces
windows with her hands in the air—
His face, just his face sticking through
the shroud, she says,
                              and I think
of the round steaming spot of marrow
in the cooked leg of lamb when he
crouched to the ground
                              and tapped
his palm hard to the joint, the strip
of singed blood slipping from
sliced bone
                    onto the bread where
he spread and rolled it. And she says,
I just held his face, then bends, cups
her hands in her lap.
                              I imagine
his face like this, sticking from
muslin like an oval flowerbed, like
the silver cover
                    of a samovar, like water
in an open teapot, or fire from his lighter
or the tip of his burning cigarette, clover-
shaped
          like *noon-nokhodchi,* or halved
pistachios on *baklava,* almonds
in *halva,* the rounds of *gaz* white
in the tray,
                    glowing like crescent
moons, my mother holding all this
in her hands, and I think, *How*
beautiful.

Sitting in bed, I can't
imagine Grandfather dead. Nothing
dies in places we've left behind.
Mother's hands
                    shade her knees.
Darkness drops its light over
the balcony where she sits alone,
thousands of miles from home.

'

Outside the Mosque

A man rolls
in his blanket, knit of old dresses,
coats, brown wool, and goat, pieces
and piece, and pieces. Old lives.
His ear to wool, he listens:
We are all used.

The Meanings of Names

i.

      The boy was unlucky—
Mother says the name Massoud
means happy, fortunate, prosperous,
but Massoud drowned in liquor, died
by the shores of the Caspian, a salt
shaker in his hand. There were rumors
of suicide. Mother says no one really knows
what this young son of Amoo Reza,
the Sufi-loving, opium-smoking, eldest
brother of my cautious grandfather,
really did.

In the silence of my American room,
I think—my ameh's name is Massoud
too, the youngest sister of my father,
deaf and mute since age seven, survivor
of diphtheria. They executed her only
child. She died within the year. *From
a broken heart,* Mother said. His name
was Reza too, meaning resignation,
consent. I imagine her silent hands
in flight, speaking of his death, arms
gesturing his four daughters, her throat
snuffing words through the light
in her eyes.

ii.

      Amoo Reza died of the same
cancer, five days before Grandfather did.
His boy in the ground twenty-five years,

his raw throat laughing with chemicals,
his head shaped like a lightbulb, bald
from months of radiation. *At least,*
Mother says, *Grandpa didn't suffer
like that.* It was sudden, the clean knife
of surgery instead. No one there could
bear to tell him his brother was dead.
We are too connected not to care too
much for one another.

    iii.

                    In Michigan
I'm choosing a name for my son.
Mother sits on the couch and says
I shouldn't think too much. Where
I am, leaves and children appear
and disappear into fog, swallowing
the lake in and out.
            How lucky
we are at least to be moments within
one another in places that pass
with the last breaths of our names.
Out the window, the sun lights
the fog. And the sky catches fire.

    iv.

                He failed
at everything he tried, Massoud did.
Lying in a hospital bed, Amoo Reza
raised his eyebrows, said, *Lucky?
Massoud lucky? Not my son.
If someone took good luck, rolled it,
shoved it up his ass,* he said. *My son?
He'd fart it out.*

21

Appearances

When Ameh Esmat's heart
gives way, eighty years old,
seizing then trembling tight
rhythms still, Mother says, *Don't tell
your father.* How many deaths
have I known of first?
Blood pools in her heart, cools
her ribs, veins, flesh stopped.
The last time I saw her, she sat,
too old to come to the airport, too
old to even turn and look once
I left the room, she, cross-legged
on her bed by the window, white
cloth poured lightly over her
head and back like milk glass,
like one glowing, giant heart, still
on the sheet, the slow rise and fall
of her back beneath, counting.

Don't tell him, Mother says. *You
know how he cries for his sisters.
His heart will burst,* she says.
He will cry by himself. In the folds
of his hands—*I've seen it before,
when Amoo Atefat died.* His hands like
the cotton cover I imagined over
his loins. *A wisp of a man.* Skin
tanned, he asks in the garden corner
of me and my sons, although they
say he can't recall much. And I'm
not sure whether Father has told me
this, or if I imagine it—does it
make a difference?

When he asks,
I tell my son, *You came from this*
earth and you will go back to it.
We inherit each other, speak
ourselves through the skip-beats
of words.
        The dead live there.
And the dying, suspended.
In Isfahan, children pass
with trays of fruit, candy,
and tea at the grave in exchange
for blessings and prayers. I am
not there to see the sun burn dry
silver webs of dew, squeeze blades
of grass, the stones, the slow
disappearances of those beneath.

How to Cut

  Home from the bazaar
Grandfather first washes his hands
with alcohol, saying, *The hands,*
the hands, Susie joon, are the dirtiest
parts of the body—you must wash
them very well. Dirty? *Do we not*
pray with our hands? I ask. *And that*
is why, he responds, *they must be clean.*

My grandfather, the only member
of our family whose English is fluent,
tells the same Churchill jokes again
and again—I don't have the heart to tell
him he's told them before. The currency
he carries must be new, unbent. In three-
piece suits and Stetson hats—only made
of wool—a gold watch chain hanging
from his vest, only cotton on his back
for shirts, wool for coats. He cuts his old
hats in pieces before he throws them out.
Did he believe another's head where his
once was would steal his soul? Or did he
find it simply unclean? Would that
hat take memories with it? Or is it
that the spaces thoughts fill are sacred?

Not knowing why, Mother now cuts
almost everything. She's a serious cutter
of old bills, letters, socks, underwear,
even pants, and when she cuts I see
his hands snipping the old Stetson into
triangles, squares, long lopsided circles,

rectangles, rhombi, and any odd shapes—
the scissors' points poised, at the ready,
rising and falling in wafts of alcohol air.

Agha Rashid Breathes In,

says, *Nothing from God is nothing.*
What do I do with these? she asks,
passing the wool shapes from one
hand to the other. *These are good*
for nothing, she says.

                  She's trimmed
bigger pieces to squares and stitched
them to a quilt. And throws
the extras into air, lets pieces
fall on his head and shoulders, like hats.
She thinks, *Nothing from God*
is nothing.

Nina Hears

Esmat Khanoom trips
on the roof, the balls of her feet tapping
the tar like a single line of rain.
What does she look for in the dark?
Does she leave tracks? The tar
is that hot. She does not. Not like
the corners of the frame Nina presses
into her nightdress, half on the cloth
half in her chest, Grandfather's smiling
face, the one she snatches from her lace
doily, clutches in bed, cries into. Why
is my daddy joon dead? Why not
someone else's? Nina hears circles
of light fall from the roof onto her
window, a lantern taking the jagged
stairs that drop without rails along
the side wall. She's still not tall, they
say, although fifty-seven, still like
a child who cannot tell the difference—
death or only dreams of heaven.

The Memory of Cells

              Grandfather, memory
must be subatomic. The cells remember
when the tumor blooms, choking silent
the neck where only darkness once
breathed through and through, a sore heart
seething in the ribs of your throat, a seed
hanging by one root, an *albaloo* fruit.
That tiny red thought—it's chromosomal.
The cells—they remember all the dark
passageways of the body. I carry your
dying inside me like this,
              remembering
your first symptom—unable to swallow—
when you swallowed all your life *mast-e*
sadeh, hoping to keep doctors away,
swallowed all that lean beef and lamb,
sure to cut the fat off first, no liquor,
no drugs. What good did it do? I

remember your never setting heels
on the street of anyone you even
suspected had cancer. As if you could
breathe the sickness in—we all have
our superstitions. I think, *Don't tempt*
the body, this,

              when I force
my legs to jog down our suburban
Michigan streets, far from the hot tar
Tehran smells of your house, of wet
asphalt, your body, your soap, force
myself through echoes of your voice

praying, through lake effect heat, wind,
sleet, fog, whatever, as if running
from the bone-baring paring knife,
bowls full of marrow, and I'm sure I
know how I will die, the pull of thighs,
tearing through tangles of leaves.
Walls cluster quiet midwestern homes
toward the lake while the future courses
through the beating heart, over, and over,
keeping time.
                    Pushing through blue
burning water, to sky, through torn seams
of membranes, we burst from the deep,
dark black mouth of memory.

Nina Calls

And Esmat hears, but
cannot speak, the garden hose cut
and wrapped around her neck,
working the flesh with markings
that leave red welts for weeks. She
chokes a sound, struggles, the edges
of the hose hanging sharp behind
her back where he stands and tightens
again, squeezing her throat. And I think,
Was this how it felt for Grandfather in the end?
Nina, irate, stops waiting, comes
out to complain from her bedroom,
sees Grandmother's legs kick
the corner window. And when
Nina sees her stockings, the man behind
Grandmother, garden hose in one hand,
carpet blade in the other, crazed
eyes, she screams. And screams.
And screams the kind of scream
that outdoes any house alarm,
the scream that begins in the dark
deep of the uterus and climbs
the body for air, from the black
throat of the earth to the rocks,
to the roses, to the street, through
the city, to the mosque, to the sky,
and into heaven where she imagines
Grandfather, even, will hear
the intruder jumping the wall
and scampering past the wild dogs,
a neighbor in pursuit who never
catches him, the rest of the neighbors

bursting from their doors, climbing
the gate, the walls, pouring out like
molten steel, while Nina screams and
Grandmother lies on the asphalt, alive,
her legs limp, her stockings marked
with mud, the water still running,
rolling dirt bubbling around the roses.
And they all look at Nina, the way
her round thighs press together, pinching
her dress in between, a tiny mountain,
bashful, often called Unwell, Crazy,
A Terrible Pain, who is now quiet.
They think what they never thought
before: *Thank God*
for Nina, Mother says. Thank God
there is always an ear listening
in the silence.

Why They Attacked

        Esmat Khanoom?
The desperation of the poor? The stupor
of drug addicts? Or the entrepreneurs
who want the city land for a new
apartment building?
                        Grandmother's
Afghan neighbor rushed like a kite
over the walls and into the streets,
calling *Thief!* Screaming *Thief!*
Thief! but no one cared to hear
or believe.

Bars

Grandmother and Nina live
in tandem, two birds in a cage,
I think, *At least they're the same*. Even
the windows, barred and rigged.
The house alarm tripped off,
everyone turns crazy. The shrill
sounds send Nina screaming
her own alarm. Grandmother hops
in her kitchen in tight circles.
*Esmat Khanoom?! Esmat
Khanoom?!* the neighbors yell,
already out. When Father finds
the off-switch, everyone scours
for the intruder, tromping
around the house, flinging open
shower curtains, checking
under beds, the men tearing
open closet doors with James
Bond precision. Grandmother,
once alone with Mother, quiet, holds
up the spatula, then says, *Perhaps*

*they ask me what I think of iron
bars. For around the house,
you know. To keep Grandma
safe.* I think of the fear that has made
her want to be rid of the house,
watering the flowers, always
remembering the shadow behind
her, how someone is hired
to be with her every hour of every
day—even Ghossam, the ten-year-old

Afghan boy who gets the night shift,
sleeps on her dining room floor next
to the back doors. A cigarette
between her fingers, Grandmother
begs everyone to take the boy home.
I don't need him here. He snores.
He screams in his sleep.

       Nina still
lies nervous in her bedroom, comes
out a few times a night to check
on her mother and pace in front
of the barred windows, the cats
outside screaming into morning.
Since the war, she's given up
sleeping outside. Since Great-
Grandfather died, she seldom
walks outside at night. Since
Grandfather died, she no
longer sleeps well at all.

Nina sits at her glass cabinet and
rearranges her figurines, one next to
the other, arm to snout to ear,
turning them into walls. Outside,
the iron at her window bars darkness.
Ghossam dreams in the next room.
Grandmother smokes. I will build
my own walls, she may think, the chirp
of glass clinking glass, the only
sounds in the house.

II: Lovers

I am a child. Love is my teacher,
waking me from ignorance.

Like Love, I will live on,
radiant, eternal,
when eating and sleeping are done.

—Rumi

The Anatomy of Hands

You fill my arms
with purple veins of dawn-lit clouds. Inside
my night-dark house, I walk through spaces
you've left on the third step of my living
room stairs, your hands held there, where
I stand, watch through the places you sat,
waving the past back into my house, your
hand at my back, my ribs. If hands
are defined by what they carry, mine
are filled with your moonlight.

And I will
hold this darkness at my palm's center
while you tell a breeze our secret. This
morning still dark with night, my feet sink
to freezing April sand and water of Lake
Michigan. And I will take nothing living
from you, neither fish nor hands, the bones
sinking deep to the shores of the body,
waves bent to waves, thousands of lit candles
on water, the calls of gulls outside your wind
and here again, echoing from my hands
and into your ears while the water drops again
and again like praying fingers falling to sun,
the trees, my feet wet, my pant-legs wet, small
fingers freezing through. With you, I know
I will never die.

My hands fill
with your words. And I am the ghastly foam,
that illness, the creases of skin remembering
your hair, your back, turning away, my heels
marking the distance.

I am that half-inch
icicle dripping from crests. *That small.* Breathe,
and disappear. Carve into me the deepening
layers, press into me the waters I have left—
Mediterranean, Atlantic, Lac Leman, Caspian,
Pacific. Whisper the secret of what can make
one survive separation.
                  When the sun lifts
its face, where will that sliver of moon
disappear to?
                  I am filled with your moonlight,
your face in every bend of sand, on every
cup's rim, in every fold of blanket, or drop
of bath water, or motion of thawed leaves. You
are the lift of the earth beneath, the deep purple
dripping from ice, frozen patches at my pant-legs
tapping my ankles, reminders, as I walk
through remembering your mouth, your
fingers' tips swirling to my wrist as I walk
home. And the moon whispers a secret before
it burns into sunlight.
                  If you believe this, kiss
me again, and again, and again, and once more
before. Walk back into my house. Walk back
into my house, a breeze on your tongue.

At the Airport

Friend, I understand
this much: you crushed me
open. Listen:

we are bells,
half-worlds, our mouths
hollow like a life never lived

because we were meant
that way. And because you
and I, each on our side

of the world, will knock
at these walls, no door, only
ringing, the ringing, and music

is a spinning cup full
with absence. I have
learned this much:

nothing breaks open
the heart like walking
in opposite directions.

Lovers

i.

The black wind and oak wrap each
other, lovers stealing time. Old leaves
rustle words, stir them apart, stir them
dry. Time is not the greatest distance
when their eyes show a quiet forgetting
of who they are, like the whistling train
breathing a stillness that cleans, a dying
that wraps branches of cracked sky.

ii.

He promised her a river as good
as any Montana, and the greens
she's grown are ready for rivers.
For weeks her fingers have watered
the trays, plucked roots clinging
to cheesecloth, raked the stalks
from the sun as faithfully as she could
be to her grandmother's ways. And
now she is waiting to go to her rivers.

His leaning is lit below her window,
his legs rooted beneath him. She turns
off her light to see his wrists push
the seams in his pockets. She knows
the watching that seeps with a soul
as full and steady as its waiting.
And his face fades with the white
of her walls, turns its breath home.

She doesn't need the greens she's grown
to show her what want means. She untangles
their reaching. She straightens

their leaning. She knows the old voice—
it's not the right place; it's not
the right time. The stalks, too long,
burst wet at her knuckles. Bending
is done. When ribbons fall free, water
roots where she's never seen such sun.

iii.

She has no room to pace at night, like her.
But speaks, eyes closed. She hears words
tap at the darkness, sees his paintings
hang from his hands, feels him push
at the small of her back and into his ribs.
He holds her face, and kisses it hard. He
adds more paint to her legs where there's
never enough bent to the wall. And if
he leaves, she runs from him in the hall.
She turns her greens to the river without him.

She turns in bed, the clock turns 2:00, turns
2:38, 3:15, 4:44, 6:10, 7:29. Her husband
breathes his dreams beside her. Some sun
parts his lips.
                    His wife shuffles to his
bed. They part when the shades are bright.
She sleeps, eyes opened. For her to stay,
he would need to ask the light to shade
its rising, she would need to ask the sun
to let her speak, he would need to ask
her words to shame him quiet.

iv.

She birthed his sons last night
in her bed between the crimson
folds. She pulled them from herself,

41

one, then the other, holding below
their necks. While her husband
smiled his sleep, she birthed hers.

She heard his music playing names.
Were songs the names he gave
her sons? She had no time to name.
Their heads stirred her shoulders

awake. Their eyes, like his, their
hands, like his, faded. The shades
emptied their light, emptied her arms,
her sheets, her legs dried, husband
stirred, her breast, aching with milk,
leaving sleeping births set to song.

v.

If someone asks what friendship is,
smile and say, it is not enough. If
someone blames the moon for never
speaking, tell him or her, listen again.
If she ever wishes he never loved
her, look again for her footsteps
wet at his door. Lilacs star
the sky lavender. Water stripes
her coat. In the upstairs window
his shoulders slice the panes.
And if the moon should drop from
its white space, if it rolled at her
feet, she would lift it from this rain
and give it back to the empty sky
above his house, above his face.

vi.

The soul lives there in the silent breath.

When one has lived a long time
without, there is a blue burning
for. To look at the red and black
of her life pulled strong like canvas
over her bones, you'd think she'd
learn to live with distance, learn
to breathe the quiet that fills souls.
But she breathes blue. To tell him so,
she would need words louder than
the silence between them.

Eid Mobarak

In Celebration of Spring

I could cut your form
in a lily's red, a black
stroke of the pallet knife
in the petals speckled
and peeled open, bent
back by the sun, and show

how you sprinkled lentils
in trays of water, covered
the seedlings with cloth
until the shoots uncurled
and pushed through wisps,
how you tied the sprouts

with ribbon as they grew.
I could shape your skin
on the canvas, white
in the bells of a hyacinth,
and remember the sweet
scent of your arm folded

around my shoulders,
arranging the apples,
the bowl of saffron,
garlic cloves for Eid,
explaining which piece
was for joy and which

was for luck in the New
Year as you brushed
and circled your fingers

in spice. I should speckle
your fingertips yellow
with pollen, handing
the bud to a small girl

waiting, her lips parted,
pretending to dab them
red and paint her mouth
as if it were the lily stuck
in the vase, dying in water

with hyacinth, waiting
for spring to come.
I would crown you
with a wreath of ivy
and call you Queen
of the Garden, as you

pulled the knotted roots
matted to the shape
of the tray, ready to throw
the ribboned sprouts
in the steam at Eid
in celebration of spring.

My hands hang white
and thin and round; a pearl
drop of azalea spreads
the oil, cuts your shape
in stamens, strokes
and strokes your skin.

Vessels

someone untied your camel last night
For I hear its gentle voice
Calling for God in the desert
—Hafiz

Look inside: I am the dark
well. You, the water.

Water,
       love the bucket
that lifts you free.

              Well,
love the emptiness that is
your hollow body.

Bucket, be slow, be
shallow, and rent

with holes so wide, moons
slip through you.

Bucket, untie the knot
of your rope, and be

the gunwale of a boat
floating on its side.

Hunger

My grandfather's wool
cashmere coat hangs in the guest
closet of my damp hall, from Tehran
to Georgia, the light shining only on
its left shoulder when the door cracks
open. This morning I've found night
halos of mold around the bedroom
vents. The blooms tuft on the Persian
twists of my rug, freckle my closet suits
in the front, swarm on their dark backs,
and when I check the guest closet I see
the right shoulder of Grandfather's coat
silvered like a bristled chin.
                            Grandfather,
the mold finds you even here. Your coat
that I begged for, your coat, sewn from
the finest English fabrics, that you stashed
in your closet, meticulous, God knows how
many years you saved it and why, but
after your death they found it with five
thousand dollars, new bills, our letters
and photos, and all manner of documents.
But I have the coat, from Grandmother, in
my closet now, where the mold has set
in, where I stand and choke back
rage.

I have found these
tufts of hunger for days on my rugs,
on my porcelain toothbrush holder, soap
dish, skirts, and pants, and I'm checking
all the closets daily for more growth. I tell
my friend, *It's like holding a lantern*

to my things, the mold-light dropping
in concentric circles, and each day I find
the decay of colors in my home, dulled
by the tiny halos of darkness that need
feeding.
            And Grandfather, I think of all
that starves, my bare feet on the rug
in every home I've lived in,
now wet with Georgia humidity,
and I wonder if hunger is the tie
that binds, because we are all walking
this earth starving for something, we are
all living blossoms of hunger, eating
at each other. When I am told the mold
grows from beneath the house, I imagine
its round edges reaching like hands
up the walls, into windows, over our
beds, our bodies, covering, smothering
the circle of my mouth, riding my breath
to the words that sit at the round pits
of my lungs, my throat, my children,
my house, until we all become one mass
of digestion.
                    While we sleep, this world
grows in every dark, dank corner
of every house, not the slow decay
of a Tehran cemetery, or even
the freezing black passageways
of Georgia's air-conditioned vents
but the quick snap starvation
of feet with nowhere to travel,
of the living when wrapped tight,
pockets empty, body buttoned
by the relentless monotony
of satiation.

Dissecting Turtles

                    I know well the beating
heart of the turtle. And the burning
of the sawed shell is that smell in the dark
early hours of morning, when hundreds
of turtles' eyes blink beneath Georgia
clay-water, their backs humped like stones
in the lake bed, hundreds of hearts cupped
inside. I know well the live snapping
turtle we dissected in pre-med physiology,

the rotary saw screeching deep into its speckled
shell. How, even paralyzed, spine pithed
at the neck, the turtle fought. Rocked
on its back like an unsteady bowl, its clacking
head tilting its balance, its limbs hung limp,
its neck pulled tight to the right by a white
cotton noose knotted to the silver knob of a gas
valve that jutted like a command from the lab's
black Formica. My silence slipped down

the dark hollow of its mouth that opened
and clacked shut like the steady crack
of a Bunsen burner that cannot be lit but raps
with a hard succession of sparks. I never held
the saw but bore into the night of the table, not
the snapping mouth, until the shell gave way
to an inner world of moving metals and water,
the hundreds of billions of atoms that travel
from space, to the ocean, to the turtle, to us.

We are all massed atoms of thought, each particle
in orbit around another, and I rested the whorls
of my bare fingerprint on the heart's three

chambers where I felt its tissues swell,
then squeeze, thrust and whiten. I would
think of this whiteness. For years I could
not bear the smell of hot bone. For years
I would lie in bed remembering the rope. Had
you followed me then from above those three

chambers, you might have found yourself here,
sixteen years later in my front hall, where
I stood in a dream of gold and green turtles,
hundreds appearing on my rugs, my wood,
my chairs, till I filled bags, and bags, and bags
with them, lifted and carried them
out to the grass for fear of killing them.
Because I would not willfully kill. And
because one should never strike a heart
that rushes and beats with this world.

Sestinelle for Travelers

We are bound for the silence of unknown roads
and trails winding red clay hills. And for what we bring
down the paths of this blue world. The traveler knows

the lumber trucks that sway past the mottled nose
of a stabled mare and the folding joint of a heron's wing
past corridors of mailboxes. Past every home we've ever known.
The logs they haul, like unclothed bodies, shadows
upon shadows, trembling. These trucks ring
down the paths of this blue world. The traveler knows

the fog will part when trucks push through like boats, knows
the circles of cut logs vanish in mist like dying galaxies, these rings
we are. Bound for silence of unknown roads

together we wind a universe. We feel it, know it, on these roads
where fog rises from water like heat from a body that wrings
down the paths of this blue world. The traveler knows
these are the alleys, ravines, side streets traveled all our lives,
    shadows
that hang the sun at our backs, the canopy of telephone wire
    and wings.
We are bound for the silence. Unknown roads

curve through the heat, where metal clamps of trucks corrode
and life is a falling turquoise pendant flipping from an old, gold
    string
down the paths of this blue world the traveler knows,

flipping fast, like a lit cigarette tossed from a window, where
    there is no
stopping. Bark peels, wind-whipped, as if loose skin or wings.
We are bound for the silence. The unknown roads

where strangers' oncoming cars will veer out of reach. And
    home
is crushed glass gleaming on a street, like stars. Or gold rings
down the paths of this blue world. The traveler knows

the orange flag that trembles at the end of one long trunk,
    knows
that fog won't clear from around this house. Once it clings
we are bound for silence. Unknown, rowed

logs sway, appear, and vanish down random roads,
ready for travel on trucks with smokestacks shimmering,
We are bound for the silence of unknown roads,
say the faces, lit, as they keep watch at passing windows,
their eyes, constellations blooming inside, stare sobering.
Inside our homes we lie like cradled, unlimbed shadows.

This world is ringed by many bodies pressed together. Shadows
we are bound by: the silence, the unknown roads—
down these paths—these blue worlds. The traveler knows.

Filling the Spaces We Know

for Willem de Kooning
I have to change to stay the same.

            There isn't
always space for change.
They say your last works
are sparse, emptied beauty
in your forgetting to fill
the space paint faded
with you.

            And death moves
in a space too small
for remembering, one
closing in too fast
on the hands, leaves
no room for the years
of emptied bottles,
aching back at a turned
canvas, the last scraped
stroke that folds one
ripple of cadmium red
to the white you
leave behind.

I. To My Unborn Son

                           For now,
You are the quiet knot I carry. And I am glad.
When you open your hands to the morning
Pushing its light over the scab of your navel,
Remember it marks where your mother once
Was, that I will carry always within my new
Emptiness the space you once occupied,
My kisses beneath your feet, the shadow
Of your profile at my breast as the maple
Outside our window blushes into winter.

II. To My Son at Seven Months

For now, you fill
My palms, my arms, with warm and quiet
Song. And I am glad.

When
The earth should fold my breathing
To its breast and hold me there, I would
Swallow stones, would tear its roots,
Its trees, for missing you, your face,
Your open hands spread soft and round,
Ice flowers on my throat. And I should
Always smell your breath bloom down
My folding arms, sweet, white, milkweed,
Aging, flying, from this frozen ground.

III. To My Son at Ten Months

You hold the moon
In your eye, for now, your face still
Bright with remembered sounds:
A skipped beat, red gurgle of water
Whirring of breath blue with wanting
With waiting for you. And I am glad

The moon will always lift and turn
Your hands in pointed spirals, spinning
Like windmills, twisting air. My ear
At your back, I hear oceans
Of breath, your heartbeat turning
And returning as if a thought
Just forgotten. And your voice,
Moonlit, lightens the quiet,
Exhaling night back to the sky.

Walking Home in Autumn

My hands push to my pockets.
A mile ahead, a figure
approaches, and I wonder

which of us will cross to the other
side first. The leaves turn. One whirls
its tips to the sky as if a dervish,

one hand toward God, the other
toward earth. We all
exist inside our own pockets

of emptiness. *Pour your light
into these washed palms, and I will
hold joy there like a veined sun.*

III: Continuance

Music floats on wind
like driftwood on waves.

In the ocean depths,
pearls shine, lending their beauty
but never touching the surface.

We hear their dazzling echo.

—Rumi

Tara

Perhaps it was the length of his torso or the sway
of his legs like long slow reeds against the wind, or
perhaps it was the tilt of his head when he first
greeted her, whatever it was, my cousin led
him to her bed, forgetting her husband, her child,
because this man meant more at that moment
than anything, than even the years it took
to build a life of pianos, and fine furniture,
rugs upon rugs, and silver. She must have known
he was too good for her, even then, she must
have known it watching him pore over the keys,
with Tara, teaching her which songs to play
when she was grown, must have known that
no life like his would change for a woman
like her, after all, a man like that doesn't give
his life to a woman like her, and she curses
the day they met, curses that she ever made
love to him, curses the moment she kissed
the freckles on his shoulders, curses the very
floor they stood on when he said he loved her
the first time,
        now, from a jail cell where Postars
have made her wait, now, Tara, her daughter,
in her husband's custody because that is how
it's done when a woman is unfaithful. And
the bars must look to her like the very lines
of memory, or music, or the passageways
between long legs, or the distances between
parallel lives, carefully measured, like comfort,
and obedience, and it doesn't matter anymore
what is said or what is left to be said, because
she thinks if she really tries she can make herself

61

disappear into the spaces between them, starts
by losing four pounds, then four more, so what
happens next makes no difference, and what
happens next, she's too far gone to notice,
her daughter is gone, her husband, gone, and
her lover kisses his own wife, who sits thick
with child eight months while he's unable
to shake this feeling he's responsible for
the entire world.
            Yet he can easily choose one
woman over the other, and I wonder, how
easily decisions can come to a man, when they
come so slowly to me, the world, two hands
on my shoulders, my cousin, her prison,
a rifle, or a reed, a child, or, even, God, who
says one thing I hear a long while, *I made
the moral choice.*
            I ask, *the right choice?*
when the bars, the bars are not enough to punish
us clean, to close us in, to hold us back.

At Night

Agha Jamshid fights that kind
of sleep that yawns into noon, blades
of arm hair bristling. His fingerprints
whirl red juices of cherries, cuticles,
dirt-filled cups of skin. His wife
jangles her wedding bracelets, skin
still itching, triangle tracks left
in her pale forearms. She lifts
her chador behind and over her pale
head when ready, her face the sun
in fabric folds.

               Yawning gold,
he asks, *A kilo? Half kilo?* His hands
two plums rolling apricot baskets,
peaches, melons, mangos. *No,* I say
Na. In-ha. These. His fingers prong
a pomegranate, his life lined beneath
its yellow stalks, marked mud
cavern of his palm.

               Her hands wet
with prayer, she bends her breath
at her hips, the shining cuffs of her
wrists dropping to plastic bags. I see
in her open chador, the dark crevasse
between her breasts. And I think
of the darkness between so many
spaces where wisdom finds us.

At night they sleep on their rug
and blankets behind the stand.
Agha Jamshid climbs to the roof,

smokes, may think the fruit, the woman,
the man, the moon, the sun, the darkness
within and behind this speckled dome
of our lives—it's all the same. We
are all this same smoke. In hours
he'll crawl behind her sleeping back,
gold pressing into her face. He'll unfold
himself to the rug, feel the tips of cut
threads pricking his knees, his ankles.
Perhaps she dreams of falling in love
with the sky, he thinks. Hot breath
of tobacco warms the backs of her
ears, wrists. All sounds muffled there,
arms scratched raw, freckled red.
This blood steps slowly across
her hands, and she sleeps, his breath
pressed lightly, her eyes, open.

Ghossam Sleeps

but he dreams all night
of sleeping on a bus that never
stops. His brother, in Zaranj,
his mother, father, gone.
He wonders why his brother
stayed. *You leave for nothing,*
for nowhere, he said. *Dirty*
Afghan. And Ghossam left
his bed, his head full, carried
his shoes, feet loose, snuck
to Zabol, Iran, by foot, by bus,
wheels spinning plats of dust.
At two in the morning

Esmat Khanoom rolls in the dark
blankets of dream onto her back,
the black of the room against
the window, the scent of shampoo
and fresh water, curtains swaying.
She opens her eyes. Nina's ear
is at her mouth, listening.

Who?

　　　　Nina always hears
voices, says she is pinched
when no one in the room
is ten feet close, says she
is blown on when no one
stands in the house. *Who
is it?* She thinks at night
she hears the dead moan
when she lights her lantern
to check the roses. Is it war
she hears? Do the Postars
shuffle outside her gates?
Does the thief tear a blouse
when he climbs back over
the wall to Lili's house?

A Visitor

Esmat Khanoom thinks
she hears Grandfather walking
on the roof. She takes a lantern,
lights it, floats it to the tarred top
of her house, and stands alone there,
moonlit, fire at her face, tightening
the black beads of her eyes.

Ziba Says

Nina was marked
before she was born, that spirits used
her for years. Ziba is here to clean
house, to hear how my grandparents
wanted that third child so badly
they even went to a gypsy fakir, ring
pendant and all, then conceived a third
daughter, not the son Grandfather wanted:
Nina—born with crossed eyes and a tongue
thick in her mouth, who would hear
voices, beat herself, sob for hours,
until Ziba says,
                    Lie on your stomach.
Then traces saffron along paths of Nina's
spine. Nina laughs, saffron on her
shoulders, down each line of her back
ribs, around fine hairs of her lower
torso, up to the V line of her neck,
as if it were the very road to heaven,
the secret way, she thinks, to Grandfather
from her heart to the sky. No one else
in the room. When Nina wakes,
tired, she takes her shirt and turns,
her eyes burning. In the night-
time mirror she sees her back-stained
map of gold.

In the Morning

Esmat Khanoom
finds saw marks on the iron bars
around the house, as if some giant
cat has tried to claw its way out.

Lower Manhattan

If you're lost, look for the World Trade Center,
and you'll find your way home.
        —a Passerby

        From the United Nations
International School on FDR Drive
and 25th Street, Mother and I walked
the wind north fifteen blocks to meet
Father who waited for us at the United
Nations, the Hudson River lapping
its edges, lifting our hair to the brass
of rush hour traffic. And the Twin
Towers gleamed with western sunlight
if I looked over my small shoulder.
If you are lost, look for this shining,
shadows looming over the bay
as the Staten Island Ferry pushed
its way from Lower Manhattan
through Hudson water home to
New Jersey, the skyline receding
till the towers slipped between
the closing pinch of my thumb
and forefinger, my eye just behind.
This city, in the palms of my hands,
beneath spaces of clamped fingers,
where I carried it to France, Iran,
Switzerland, Texas, Nebraska,
Michigan, where I still hold it,
the years I've left behind. How
will I find my way home? My palms
burn. If you are lost, look

for my eyes, hot in your hands.
Carry me there, bright, burning,
and alive.

Torches

Three days and the flames gleamed
up the south wall stairs onto Esmat's
roof, forty flaming heads lifting
the night, then pulling back along
each concrete edge. Tables lined
one end of the flat tarred roof. I
remember only swinging from
clotheslines—a small, frail child.
The noon sun beat the top of
the house, honeysuckle, evenings
when Nina hummed downstairs
in her room at the open window,
her voice rising air ducts jutting
rectangular chimneys from
the tar. I am not there to see this
new roof, lit like a funeral
pyre of kabob and rice.

This fire is not the flame of luck,
the pyres they jump over in streets
at *Nowruz*. These are the lights
of those who wait, burning till
embers of forgetting, as they fill
the tables while Grandfather hovers
in the fluid space between flame
and sky. He is this shining, shimmering
space, this hot halo, this whispered
hat held over the house tipped
with forgiveness, the fire held
close, scalding the sky.

Interring the Body

              They lift
and lower his body three times
as if it were the rug he grew old
with, first born in his bedroom
then resting his feet in his living
room, now wrapped in muslin
and tied at the ankles, the waist,
the neck, rolled like thread wool
just pulled from the loom, rooted,
knotted, carried from the room
to the crowd who waits. Within
the gates, Esmat Khanoom takes
nothing. Her hands are empty.
This wasn't the plan, she stands
thinking, Nina at her left, a space
to her right, cold with his absence.

They lift him to their shoulders
the first time, and the sun moves
around the shadows of his face
a full day. The second time
they lift him to their chins, the tie
on his ankles coiled and raveled.
The third time, Nina slaps dirt
to her face, drops to the ground,
and Akbar and Siamak wait
in the grave to receive his body,
wrapped, tight, and trembling.

Continuance

What is there
in this stillness that tars the roof?
Dried blades of grass strewn
on the sidewalk promise someone
will sweep, the burst of roadside
petals will fly from under a passing tire,
a cloud of cinnamon will rush through
a sunbeam when a window blows
on hot oatmeal, hundreds of birds
at dusk folding into oceans of peppered
sky, the promise that we can never die
inside the green blade and the hand
that sweeps it, the wingtip and the wind
it rides. These small lives call, *How
is the forgetting this vast and the key
this small?*

What is true in a place
is always the history it occupies. The child
that climbs to the back seat after school,
the woman who now waits in line, remembering
the very arc of stepping into afternoons
of promised cartoons and Oreos, and humid
New Jersey hours inside the house, the sun
beating the hours into the roof saying,
*Today will lead to some place of repeated
comfort where even scars will brighten.*

Light

i.

Tehran, Iran

Against the street dark
of lamps in downtown Tehran
Muslims carry burning eyes
of candles in the hollow pits
of their hands, the arches
glowing quiet between thumb
and forefinger. *Hayfe,* Shame,
one man says. In the backyard
of Grandmother's house
the roses drink from her
palms. A stale smoke rises
from the grill, flesh still
attached. She watches the moon
lift early over the shimmering
green of leaves, and thinks,
In sha'Allah, God willing, this
world is a dream.

ii.

Zaranj, Afghanistan

Ghossam's
brother knows what will happen
now. These bombs will be worse
than the floods. He packs his only
bag with matches, apples, wheat,
almonds, water, the rounded

roof of his house moving by
like an oversized fig. He drifts
from country to country, wishes
for a time when no lines divided
them, when the land knew no
difference. His shirt checkers
his back. His heart skips and gasps
in his feet. He steps lightly
from Zaranj to Zabol. He will
lose track of the days.

   iii.

    Holland, Michigan

         Dunes burst
from the lakeshore, Michigan
cloud-smokes. My hands catch
fog, fan the driveway, swing
home, fingers, sun-fire, leaves
yellow on black. Think lit bodies
falling, ash-ridden faces.
Every image has changed
its meaning.
         Grandma joon,
tell me this is only a dream,
fill my words with your spoons
full of honey, and let my bed's
net canopy spill and tuck beneath
my mattress.
           Step into my dark
house. Leave me never
knowing light this way.

Instructions on What to Say First at a Muslim Burial

Once you position the body correctly
in the grave, place your right hand on the right shoulder
and your left hand on the left shoulder.
Your mouth close to the ears, shake the shoulders, and say this.

In the grave place your right hand on the right shoulder
Firmly. Don't look at the muslin tying the neck, waist, and ankles.
Your mouth close to the ears, shake the shoulders, and say this:
Listen —, son of —, are you holding the covenant you had when
    you left us?

Firmly, don't look at the muslin tying the neck, waist, and ankles.
Stand at his ear, your breath a tense wire on his earlobe, then say
    this:
Listen —, son of —, are you holding the covenant you had when
    you left us?
The covenant of your belief and testimony that there is only one
    God who has no partner?

Stand at his ear, your breath a length of yarn on his earlobe, and
    say this:
Sit once more before your bowl full of soap water? Will we meet
    again? Should I believe
The covenant of your belief and testimony that there is only one
    God who has no partner?
That Muhammad, His servant and Messenger, chief of Prophets,
    is the last messenger of God?

Sit once more before your bowl full of soap water? Will we
    meet again? Should I believe

That Ali, leader of believers, chief deputy of God on earth, is
    the Imam,
That Muhammad, His servant and Messenger, chief of
    Prophets, is the last messenger of God?
Then say this, *Did you Understand, Oh — of a —?*

That Ali, leader of believers, chief deputy of God on earth, is the
    Imam?
My left hand on your left shoulder,
I say this: *Will I / Did you Understand, Grandfather?*
Once they positioned your body correctly?

Where You Are

for Grandfather

       Because I breathe,
I can tell the backyard
in Grandmother's garden,
the back tooth of Nina's
yawning, the stones in Lili's
gall bladder rolling the flesh
juice into rivers. Like Mother's.
Like yours. But Grandfather,
tell me the stars. Tell me
the nowhere. Because I am still
in the universe. I breathe in
this good earth and call it
my own.

Notes

The translation of "Bani Adam" or "Sons of Adam" by Sa'adi is by Dick Davis.

Jodie Ahem, "Interview with Poet Susan Atefat-Peckham," *Poets & Writers,* online only, posted February 12, 2004, http://www.pw.org/content/interview_poet_susan_atefatpeckham.

The section epigraphs are from *Gold* by Rumi, translated by Haleh Liza Gafori (New York Review Books, NYRB Classics, 2022) (I and II, page 19; III, page 75)

The epigraph to "Vessels" is from "Someone Untied Your Camel" by Hafiz, translated by Daniel Ladinsky in *The Gift: Poems by Hafiz, the Great Sufi Master.* US: Penguin Books, 1999, 62–63.

Acknowledgments

Grateful acknowledgment is given to the editors of the journals and anthologies where these poems first appeared:

Arts & Letters: "Dissecting Turtles"
Prairie Schooner: "Clean"

"Lower Manhattan," "Night Conversations," "Sestinelle for Travelers," and "Torches" were previously published in the anthology *Let Me Tell You Where I've Been: New Writing by Women of the Iranian Diaspora* (The University of Arkansas Press, 2006).

"Tara" was previously published in the anthology *Essential Voices: Poetry of Iran and Its Diaspora* (Green Linden Press, 2021).

So much joyful love and gratitude to all the people who gave me the confidence to take on this project, especially my mentors at Interlochen Arts Academy and Harvard University: Brittany Cavallaro, Josh Bell, Jorie Graham, and Tracy K. Smith. Thank you to Persis Karim, Sholeh Wolpé, and Kazim Ali for the light of your work and your words, and for generously gifting them to this collection. Thank you to all of Susie's former peers, mentors, colleagues, and students at University of Nebraska-Lincoln, Hope College, and Georgia College.

Thank you to my beloveds in words and music, especially Isabella Farmer, Athena Nassar, Yanna Cassell, Sophie Paquette, Cookie Dutch, Helena Notario, Tawanda Mulalu, Siavash Saadlou, Sherah Bloor, Emma De Lisle, Harry Hall, Sam Bailey, Katherine Irajpanah, Vanessa Braganza, Marie Ungar, Lana Reeves, Brammy Rajakumar, Benjamin Ballet, Carissa Chen, Alex Braslavsky, Isabel Duarte-Gray, and Timothy Leo for your inspiration, kindness, mentorship, love, and warmth. Thank you to Vineet Gangireddy, Andy Kim, Cade Williams, and Bryson Parker for your assurances throughout this process, and for lending a compassionate and generous ear whenever necessary. I'm so lucky to have all of you.

Joyful gratitude to my Persian instructors, especially Sheida Dayani, Mojtaba Ebrahimian, Masoud Ariankhoo, Belle Cheves, Justine Landau, and Shahrad Shahvand for helping me learn more about Persian language and culture, and enabling me to understand Susie's work (and my own) in an entirely new dimension.

Oceans of love and gratitude to my grandparents, Bahram and Farideh Atefat (my Papa and Bibi) for loving me, for trusting me, for being two of my biggest supporters. Thank you, Bibi, for being my first Persian instructor, who passed me Persian sweets as I learned my colors and numbers at the kitchen table and incessantly repeated *Azizam, Azizam, Azizam.* Thank you for always making us laugh. Thank you, Papa, for instilling in me a love of travel and of the divine, and for keeping Susie's memory alive. Thank you for your laugh. Again: *Azizam, Azizam, Azizam.* You are dear to me.

Oceans of love and gratitude to my parents, Joel and Rachael Peckham, who supported me in this endeavor and set such a stellar example for me to follow, in life and in words. Thank you, Dad, for answering all my questions about my mother, no matter how painful. Thank you, Rachie, for reading Susie's poems with me before bed and contributing your voice to their magic. I love you both. You have no idea how much.

Thank you to all my grandparents and to my extended family, especially Joel and Jeanne Peckham, Mike and Diane Pridgeon, the Kemp family, the Maidment family, the Woodruffs, the Huyser-Pridgeons, and the Pridgeons. You all quite literally lifted me and my father to our feet after tremendous loss. It takes a village. I'm so lucky to revel in and benefit from your warmth.

Love and prayer and gratitude to all my ancestors and to the departed, especially Nina Barati, Esmat Sharifian Barati, Hasan Barati, Muhammad Atefat, and Cyrus Atefat-Peckham who breathe in many of these poems. Wherever you are, I hope you are together there with Susie.

Thank you to my Iranian family, who speak to me on the phone in Persian, whose unconditional love and passion surrounds and astounds me, especially Lili, Ezat, Sheida, Sholeh, Mustafa, and Siamak. I delight in your presence. I promise I will visit someday.

Thank you to everyone in the Iranian diaspora who have expanded my idea of *family*. I love you all.

Joyful love and gratitude to the team at CavanKerry Press for giving this collection a home, especially Gabriel Cleveland, Joan Cusack Handler, Baron Wormser, and Joy Arbor.

Joyful gratitude to Maryam Lamei Harvani for allowing us to use her beautiful piece for the cover art of this book.

And finally, joy and gratitude to all of Susie's beloveds who have told me stories, gifted me memories, and trusted me in the work of surviving her—both in poems and in this life. I couldn't do it without all of your tenderness, care, and belief. I wouldn't succeed in listing you all here, but as the dedication of this book asserts, these poems are for you. Thank you.

CavanKerry's Mission

A not-for-profit literary press serving art and community, CavanKerry is committed to expanding the reach of poetry and other fine literature to a general readership by publishing works that explore the emotional and psychological landscapes of everyday life, and to bringing that art to the underserved where they live, work, and receive services.

Other Books in the Notable Voices Series

Without Wings, Laurie Lamon
An Apron Full of Beans: New and Selected Poems, Sam Cornish
The Poetry Life: Ten Stories, Baron Wormser
BEAR, Karen Chase
Fun Being Me, Jack Wiler
Common Life, Robert Cording
The Origins of Tragedy & Other Poems, Kenneth Rosen
Apparition Hill, Mary Ruefle
Against Consolation, Robert Cording

Deep Are These Distances Between Us was typeset in Garamond Premier Pro, a fine-tuned version of Claude Garamond's original metal punches and type designs from the 16th century. In the mid-1500s, Garamond produced a refined array of book types that combined an unprecedented degree of balance and elegance, and stand as a pinnacle of beauty and practicality in typefounding.